WASH THE DUST FROM MY EYES

for Suzanne & Don,
with affection,

Nan

2/2016

WASH THE DUST FROM MY EYES

A year in the life of
John Mason

at
Fort Riley, Kansas

training U.S. Cavalry for WWI
1917

in journals and poems

by
Nana Lampton

Accents Publishing • Lexington, Kentucky • 2016

Copyright © 2016 by Nana Lampton

Printed in the United States of America

Accents Publishing
Editor: Katerina Stoykova-Klemer
Cover Art: Nana Lampton

Library of Congress Control Number: 2015951425
ISBN: 978-1-936628-38-4
First Edition

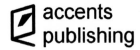

Accents Publishing is an independent press for brilliant voices. For a catalog of current and upcoming titles, please visit us on the Web at

www.accents-publishing.com

CONTENTS

Appendix

INTRODUCTION

At my mother's death, I was given the 1917-1918 diary of *John Mason,* her father, John Mason Houghland. He would have approved, since he was the one who taught me poetry when I was an adolescent girl, gave me the *Collected Poems* of the early 20th century war chroniclers Rupert Brooke and Wilfred Owen, and read Tennyson and Masefield to me. I have taken the liberty of speaking in his voice through my poems.

From my point of view, nearly a hundred years later, I found that his judgment of people from other walks of life, races and cultures, developed from disapproval, toward tolerance and acceptance. I decided to try to enter his mind and feelings as if I were the orphaned teenager handed to the world as adventurer.

In the end, he trained for war but was not sent. He kept his forward momentum using his energy to build a gas and oil distribution company called *Spur,* based in Tennessee.

Just at the end of his year of training in Fort Riley he found Sara, the woman of his dreams. She was descending the staircase in her mother's home, carrying an infant—the child of an ill-fated union. In the small town of 1918 Emporia, Kansas, it took some courage for them to leave, to leap into their own marriage.

As I imagined what he was thinking and feeling, I turned my discernment into poems.

NL

PROLOGUE

The young man already educated in literature at the University of Chicago, but also in geology and the art of wild-catting for oil joins the army before the U.S. enters WWI. He is asked to train men for the U.S. Cavalry.

Very soon the U.S. cancels the entry of U.S. Cavalry into the war in Europe and concentrates instead on artillery, so the young man is asked to train artillerymen. He is made a captain. From the hard and vast plains he is to train for war in France. But how could he even begin to think of mud and mules and caissons in that climate, and barbed wire and machine guns?

This is a story about imagination, a young man's ideas about what war would be like. How could he know, any more than a young man from Indiana could imagine war in Iraq?

I admire my grandfather's resilience, his willingness to serve, and am grateful for his fate, that he didn't have to go to France, or else I probably wouldn't exist.

NL

ORIGINS OF WAR

O foolish race of mortals, that gave gods such jobs to do,
Then went and made them fierce with anger into the bargain too!
What groans you purchased for yourselves, what grievous injury
For us, what tears you fashioned for the children yet to be!
It is not piety to cover up your head for show,
To bow and scrape before a stone, or stop by as you go
At every altar, flinging yourself upon the ground face down,
Lifting your palms at the gods' shrines, nor piety to drown
Altars in the blood of brutes, nor to chain prayer to prayer;
Rather, to look on all things with a mind that's free from care.

For when we lift our gaze to the vast precincts of the skies
And see the aether spangled with sparkling stars, a wild surmise
About the pathways of the sun and moon enters the mind,
And in the heart already gravely charged with fears, we find
Something begins to rear its head: a new Unease awakes—
Whether that unbounded power of the gods that makes
The bright stars run their various courses govern us on earth.
The mind staggers with doubt when we're faced with the utter
dearth

Of answers to our questions: did this world once have a birth?
And is there a fixed span of time the world's walls can remain
Before they give way from the unceasing motion and its strain?
Or have those walls been granted by some supernatural force
The strength to last, and slip along forever on Time's course,
Shrugging off immeasurable Age, its crippling might?

LUCRETIUS
Translated by A. E. Stallings

PREPARING FOR WAR

When it seemed unquestionably sure that Congress should declare War, Wright and I left Independence, Kansas, where we were making Field Headquarters while looking over the shallow oil country in East Kansas, and made a trip to Fort Leavenworth to find out how we could be of service and secure the training necessary for the Army. This was done on Friday of the week before war was declared upon Germany.

I returned to Tulsa, straightened up my affairs, packed my business correspondence, books, etc. closed up my office (in the Culberson Bldg. corner 4th and Main); procured a letter from Frank Frantz, late Captain 1st M.S. Volunteer Cavalry (the *Rough Riders* of Spanish American War fame) and from several of my old classmates at West Point (to whom I wrote).

I had but a few weeks before I bought a pony from Cunnert Soldani, an Osage Indian at Kaw City, Oklahoma, and had him ridden over, some 120 miles by a cow-puncher from the Soldani outfit. This pony I had been breaking for polo and hated to give him up.

Being unable to sell him because of lack of time and because of his rather lively propensities for devilment, I left him with my good friend Fred Peek, who needed some riding to get into better condition.

Then I returned to Fort Leavenworth where I spent about a week studying. While there I lived at the Officer's Club. This was in a musty old brick building, and the general atmosphere was rather picturesque, though inclined to develop lonesomeness. High ceiled dark rooms hung with pictures (prints) of Russian war scenes as done by the French artists of the '70's [1870's], and with fierce looking old Civil War Generals and Indian War Colonels whose drooping moustaches still evidenced the martial manner that had once surrounded these doughty veterans.

Never having been a student, and not having pretended any scholastic effort for five years, I found Military Law, Cavalry Drill Regulations, etc. to be very tiresome reading indeed, and longed for a more active preparation.

Finally I decided to go out to Fort Riley, where the Mounted Service Schools were located, and see if I might not find some more valuable and active preparation for a cavalry commission.

This decision opened the Gates of Paradise for me and allowed me to enter that land which Semitic folklore insists is flag-stoned with gold and chased in silver. In this case it happens to be more upon the lines laid out by the American Indian—hills, rivers, hunting and horses.

JOHN MASON

Fort Riley

Bunk room

**Learning to ride
in the Cavalry**

**Fort Riley
U.S. Cavalry School**

BY THE STREAM
A Supplication to the Four Directions

To my help from the north, white wings, be strong support.
To outer sunlight in the east, be my inner sight.
To south, rock, dog, earth, flower, Mother, give me strength.
To the west, my life to come, you ash tree,
guardian of the way with down-turned mouth, be glad.
Your wooded cliff no longer blocks my view of destiny.
By the impenetrable trees is open river, flowing south.
I choose to float the current's way.

NL

I arrived early in the morning in April 1917, introduced myself at Post Headquarters and was heartily welcomed (owing no doubt to the fact that I was about the first tangible evidence that the officers here had that civilians wanted to train.)

Captain Martin proved to be a most delightful and interesting character. He is a man of gentle eye and slow speech, simple and almost boyish in manner. His quarters would have served as an illustration in a popular periodical of all American heroes. The mantel was covered with silver cups of all kinds, won at horse shows and steeplechases, and the walls were hung with pictures of polo teams, hunt races, thoroughbred horses, etc.

There was a generously filled bookcase whose well-thumbed volumes dealt mostly with history, or were *sets* of the works of accepted writers. In the entry-way there hung a lot of polo mallets, upon the hall tree there rested several well-worn riding crops, in the bedrooms were spurs enough for a battalion.

Captain Martin is perhaps among the most highly finished horsemen in the world and has much Army fame also as a winner of steeplechases and gentlemen's events of the kind.

Incidentally he is an example of what a man from the ranks may accomplish.

Captain Palmer Swift is the active instructor at the School of Equitation and is a typical West Pointer: alert, confident, terse, and efficient. He drives hard for results and gets them. To see the two platoons of Non-Coms now taking the course make a cross-country ride is a wonderful sight. 43 riders over a three-mile course in which lay 15 obstacles, fences, stone walls, Swedish jumps, Irish jumps, etc. Every man sitting easily in the saddle, and every horse jumping smoothly and well. A sight worth going miles to see! Thanks to Captain Swift, I am getting a wonderful lot of training which I shall attempt to profit by.

Horses:

Chiswell:	Big sorrel presented to Government by Belmont. White stockings, white blaze. Ideal hunter.
Watch Me:	Black. White markings. Wonderful jumper. Ex-bolter. Only Captain Swift can ride him.
McClure:	Great jumper, always ready, stands with hind legs crossed.
Joe McAndrews:	Fine

May 5th:

Two Reserve Officers, 2nd Lieutenants from St. Louis, arrived today. They look like Grammar School children by comparison but they evidently have the right stuff and will make good officers in time.

The 2500 designated for this Officers' Training Camp have made applications and been accepted. They will begin to arrive next week. Thanks to the U-Boat efficiency the country appears to be waking up and to be beginning to realize that it is at war.

May 9th:

Moved from Arnold Hall Quarters No. 1 and was assigned place in barracks #1 just west of Post Headquarters. Left then on leave until Monday for Cherryvale to drill in O'Leary well.

May 12th:

Reached Fort Riley and went into Company #1, Captain Kinney (Regular Army) in command.

May 13th:

Went to Junction City with *Sandy Sellers* and spent the day. His wife and baby daughter there.

May 17th:

Company organized. I was made a corporal and my troubles began after the fashion of *Si Klegg* of Civil War fame.

The first reveille one student officer was prevented from attending by a sad accident. He had hung his trousers up in his locker the night previous and locked same. In the morning he could not find the key!

May 30th:

Memorial Day. Rain of course.

October-November 1917

We discover a Denver country club chef in the draft in the mess and prepare to start the 111th Battalion Mess.

JOHN MASON

John Mason

John Mason

Fresh horse

THE CAPTAIN TAKES SUNDAY LEAVE

I

Sunday leave, I wander paths between the hard granite buildings.
Whatever wind tries to dictate my life moves these flying clouds.
The careful regulations fool us into thinking
everything is ordered, the days the same.
How that would change with horses loaded
in the ship beneath my bunk, all tossed in
Atlantic crossing's wretched weather.
When we land, it's action, *then,* on the spot,
no time to read the landscape, practice how to handle
movement on the roads. Horses swim ashore.
On march we meet fleeing villagers, herds of stock
Push against our passage, jam the only roads.
Mud on both sides of the bridge.
The kind that sucks you to China.

II

Thirty thousand horses shipped from England counter
General Von Kluck at Liege. Cavalry officers, with freshly sharpened
swords, keep social standards high. General French
believed in brave assault with officers on horses,
would not submit to General Joffre's need
for reconnaissance by cavalry,
the urgent need to know where German advance would be.

Getting a start on war, I teach horses how to jump —
trenches, fences, barbed wire—but not six feet of it.

III

I was made an officer, a big step from enlisted.
Moved from barracks to quarters on my own.
Awarded *George Rodney,* my Captain's horse,
he is my own fellow teacher.
We can't teach mud in a dry plain,
nor can I teach them to run through machine gun fire,
but fitness, jumping, endurance, yes.
Maybe common sense.

NL

August 15th:

At Reveille we were a troop of officers, no longer recruits. We were all exuberant to feel the summer was over. It had been a hard one indeed and the drawn lines of each man's face were at last relaxed. Most of the conversation was of home and drinking. Although king alcohol is soon to die, he had as many friends in the army as ever before.

I was made a Captain: the fourth ranking of the prospective regiment. Looking back at the 180 men who entered, and at the thirteen who were made captains, I was dazed to think how it all came about.

It is sweet indeed to have a lifetime ambition realized and I am glad to feel that I have been fortunate enough to gain such an opportunity for service.

John Mason's Military Status

164th Depot Brigade-Camp, Funston, Kansas
342nd FA
315th Cavalry Russell, Wyoming 71st F.A.
John Mason is 29 years old.
He wrote in his journal,
Captain J. M. Houghland, U.S.M.A., West Point, N.Y.
Mounted Service School, Fort Riley Training Camp

AUNT CORDELIA TO JOHN MASON

Your father told you, you trust too much.
You believe the generals. French and Milner
for the British, Joffre for the French,
Von Kluck of Germany, speak of themselves
as well-schooled nobility, a notch under *all-knowing,*
bred of kings with better boot legs, finer noses,
better posture in the saddle.

Look at the results! They make their private decisions, so jealous
they won't consult. One army passes another allied army
in the night, by mistake, squandering troops' energy,
too late to reach the battle, to hold the line.
Soldiers march twice the needed distance.
Infantry—the lowly troop—lacks water, rest, and food,
expected to fight next morning. (This happens, I read,
more than once.) Exhausted soldiers die, wounded are left
behind—the victims of generals' bull-fighting.
Joffre fires 58 generals.

For glory of the battle, the lances and the pennants fly,
horses leap the shell holes, until they, too, are
hanging their heads for lack of food and water.
Fodder follows a week late, across the sea, then by rail.

Look, John Mason, we have to stop this insanity!
Listen! You're not any better bred than the fellows who
can't speak the language, than recruits who
might be born a different color.
Pay attention! Find the meaning of your life.
You are training first generation boys.
Teach them to go forward as Americans,

with respect and common sense. One of them
could be President one day. Try not to lose him.

NL

BARRACKS

Long, narrow, high ceiling, windows down one side. Rows of narrow white iron beds (foot to the aisle) down each side. Chorus of deep breathing, now and then a groan or snore. The cold light of early morning begins to creep into the room. From the distance comes the faint sound of a bugle—*First Call.*

A man turns over quickly, then another and another stirs. One sits on the side of his bed, another shouts at a youthful sleeper or two who have not reacted to the summons.

Leggins are laced, belts and bayonets donned and out the men stumble, each taking his *piece* (gun) from the circular rack in the aisle as he passes.

Fall in commands the Top Sargent [*sic*]. There is a momentary shuffling, a glance to the right, and the ranks waver into shape. Successively each corporal reports for his squad. *Inspection arms! Post arms! Dismissed!* Chants the *Top* and back to bedmaking come the men.

May 31st:

The bunk to my right is occupied by Paul Bush, a watchmaker from Carrolton, Missouri. Paul is 23, clear-eyed, sincere, and eager to do his part. Also he is in love with a girl from a neighboring town and hears from her <u>every day</u>. A *nice* lad of the sort that are killed or shattered by the thousands every day across that water.

Beyond him is C. L. Graham, 25, a young lawyer from the same town. Graham is fat, sleeps at every opportunity, and has a full share of Missouri complacency. Both he and Bush represent the settled, sane, orthodox middle west admirably.

On the other side is a cigarette fiend from the Colorado militia, name unknown. *Bootlicker* type. Apologies every night because he didn't bring his pajamas. I daresay he never owned a toothbrush—say nothing of night clothes.

Across the aisle is Lieutenant Rollins, a reserve officer from Columbia, Missouri, lawyer by profession. Quiet, unassuming, well-bred. The remainder of the room inhabited by Colorado militiamen whose chief topic is the feminine frailties of the border women. They have just returned from the Mexican border and their conversation needs expurgation.

One of theirs is a man of about forty, a veteran of the Spanish American War and not a bad sort. Simple and untutored, born to be a non-com. Had typhoid fever during the Spanish American war in a field hospital and describes the horrors of those days with a naïve clearness. One of the type who gravitates to *soldiering*. Later, *turned out* to the ranks again.

Darley rides up on mare followed by colt. Dismounts and regales the darkies in the co. kitchen with statement of his extensive farming operations and responsibilities. Cavalry Captain on a good-looking hunter; his little son on a bay pony; colored orderly riding some yards to the rear.

Is the colt half or three-quarters? asks the Captain pulling up.

Three quarters, answers the darkey proud to be noticed, and the two horsemen engage in conversation for some time upon the colt's breeding. True bit of horseman comraderie! Black or white, they are all in the fraternity.

JOHN MASON

May 31st, 1917:

There is to be no cavalry organized, and together with several others, I am disconsolate. War without spurs is a dull drudgery I am sure.

Now that the horses are eliminated, the last vestige of glamour is gone, and I expect nothing but unpleasantness—which is as war should be. As a form of sport it is high time it was superseded by cross country riding and polo.

The horror of the trench idea weighs on everyone. There is none of the foolish bravado one hears existed before other fights this country engaged in. The atmosphere is serious, masked by the natural enthusiasm of good health.

It's duty, not desire, with everyone I think.

JOHN MASON

Tents

Out training

Watch

Lined up

SUNRISE

... there is a separate power in distinct things ...

—Lucretius (Translated by A. E. Stallings)

Would you look at that sunrise over the edge of earth,
carmine with the full moon opposite, going down to China?
I will let the day pull me along. In the saddle, out for the day,
with exercises, gallops, charges, and field artillery until night.
I will surely sleep. But look at this! If I weren't training here
for war, I wouldn't have been witness to this morning sky.
Destiny brought me. I am not a warlike man.

NL

"Don't answer *yoh* to your names," admonishes our *Top* Sargeant [*sic*], Edwards, a Cockney of Boer War experience: "Say, *'ere, 'ere!*" When he comes to the H's at roll call: " *'ackney, 'oughland, 'utton,—*"

He has been a Captain of Police in Kansas City, then a Superintendent of some office buildings. Typical better class of Cockney: loves soldiering, refers to company as *my men;* visibly pleased when those unaccustomed to military etiquette call him *Sir* and *bootlick* him. Withal, an efficient, cheery soul blessed with plenty of common sense.

June:

The bayonet seems to be the only thing about the war that impresses the men with horror. Hardly a man but comments frequently upon the knife.

The instruction in how to stab a man repulses all: *Don't thrust the bayonet no more than 4-6 inches or you will have trouble pulling it out of the flesh.*

If you have difficulty in withdrawing the bayonet, discharge the piece; or place your foot on the man and twist the blade slightly.

Have a partner or two or three, attack one man together when possible.

At this last injunction, all men at the conference gasped. Throughout their lives they had been taught fair-play and here they were being coached for first degree murder of the *Black Hand* variety.

Bill Butler (32 Co.) a giant of an athlete was expressing his fear of the bayonet the other night, and as he spoke I wondered what some bespectacled, scholarly, little German boy would think when Bill loomed as his antagonist.

JOHN MASON

SQUAD ROOM AT NIGHT

Dim light from row of high windows shows two long rows of iron beds foot to foot. You would imagine that with all the men asleep quiet would reign. It doesn't.

Two or three men are snoring loudly and in different keys. A boy in the center of the room is talking in his sleep.

Squads go on! he mumbles, the day's drill tangled in his mind. The snores continue. A little lull. At the far end of the room a man suddenly shouts savagery at nothing, and a half a dozen sleepers turn over nervously. Then a late arrival tip-toes in. *Lightly there,* growls an awakened one. The late arrival blunders into the gun rack and swears sorrowfully. Four or five awaken and complain bitterly about the noise. The silence falls and the snoring is resumed, tremolo stops pulled out.

JOHN MASON

LOOSE MEDITATION

Wouldn't go to war without a horse, wouldn't go alone.
Trot, trot, trot, trot. One mile. Walk, walk, walk, walk.
This is where they fought the Red Man. What a shame.
Crow squawk. Walk. Then it meant something to go
a distance. They never went out for nothing, wasting
fodder and man food. Air past my face, then wind.
They would have known what weather would follow—
hot to cool in this flat land. The hawk rides the thermals
up high where he can see Europe, Paris, so long the object
of German conquest. They grabbed it, as they did in 1870.
War every fifty years? Or less. Cezanne kept to himself.
Paris was remade to be ripped up again.
They grow boys every twenty years for war.

A stream lined with cottonwoods, shade and shelter for birds,
for me. Is there a shelter for my heart? Someone who cares
if I go to war? Unknown as my fate in war, a woman meant for me.

Lucretius asks my question, *What is our nature?*
Not altruistic, I say. These men don't think.
That man wants my horse, another envies rank,
wants my job.
Fair and red-headed, they call me *Red.*

My brain refused the math at West Point, I was
excused. Lucretius understands the atom, attraction
of matter to mass. He ferrets out the secrets
of the cosmos. I emulate his courage:
citizens who read his book were burned alive.
His 7000 lines of poetry did not begin with *God.*

When war threatened, the heads of state were on vacation.
Tsar in the country, Kaiser on a yacht, others out hunting—

they couldn't be reached by messengers. Generals,
aspiring to medals, began the war, for glory.
German cavalry rode out in August 1914:
in gray-green with black-and-white pennants
fluttering from their lances like horsemen riding out of the Middle Ages.

That was August 20th, 1914. This is 1917. Now the British General Haig
rides out every day with his British pennants flying,
followed by a two-hour lunch with wine and *foie gras,*
they say. Fearing the sight of death in trenches, he never goes to see.
At Loos they died for an inch, all sixty-one thousand.
Hard to think of my surviving that.

NL

MORTALITY AND THE SOUL

Now pay attention here:
I tell you mind and spirit are bound up with one another,
And that together they combine to form a single nature.
But what heads the whole body and reigns over it like a king
Is Judgement, which we also name the 'mind' or 'understanding'
And this keeps its abode in the mid-region of the chest.
Here is the place that fright and dread stampede, here also rest
Soothing joys, so this is the region where the judgement stays.
(The remainder of the spirit, seeded throughout the flesh, obeys,
And a mere nod or signal from the mind puts it in motion.)

The mind is thoughtful by itself, rejoices on its own
When nothing agitates the flesh and spirit.

LUCRETIUS
Translated by A. E. Stallings

RUMORS

Weird tales of all kind float around camp. Somehow soldiers seem to be constantly *hearing the latest.*

> *The cavalry troop will be trained as machine gun outfits and sent to France at once.*

> *Payments of troops are all to be made in gold, and a huge stack of gold is now at the P.M.'s with marble guards around it.*

Since plans are so frequently changed by sudden orders from Gen. Barry at Chicago, it is assumed that anything may be ordered at any time.

> *So and so is under surveillance as a German spy suspect.*

> *Gen. Pershing is a 'grand-stand player' and cares nothing for the comfort and health of his men, and such rank rumors pass and re-pass as though the camp were a convention.*

> *Aaron Burr whispered seriously to an attentive group. Wednesday*

> *Fellows I have it direct that tomorrow will be—<u>Saturday</u>!*

June:

No army for me when this war is over. I feel sorry for army officers, they lead so quiet a life, announces a gentle-voiced little Irishman in 2 Company.

It turns out that he is originally from New York, enlisted in the Artillery at 15, served two enlistments and for six years has been a fireman in Kansas City. Is quite sure that a fireman's job is the most attractive on earth, but of course if there is war it never occurs to him that he shouldn't be among the first in it.

Pays suit to a Jewess in Kansas City and her people think him to be a Jew. Seems fascinated by their attitude towards life—it is so strange to him.

First thing they talk of is <u>business</u>, he earnestly informs you. To him, with fires, and armies, and vaudeville shows and the police court dramas, business seems an odd subject to mention socially. (I think that after all he is right.)

Told Sellers and me of saving a painted woman from a fire: carried her down the ladder from third story and was burned considerably by intervening flames. The next day attempts a bit of illicit love affair with her and to his never-ending surprise is repulsed.

Wouldn't that stagger you? he says.

Newspaper clippings are joy unbounded to him. To be mentioned in a line he would twice chance death I am sure.

Not conceited nor unpleasant: simple, natural sort of man, of true Irish type such as depicted in *The Playboy of the Western World*.

JOHN MASON

A LONG DAY TRAINING

A long day across the prairie, riding for hours in formation.
Look at the light cape the shoulder of this fit horse. It radiates from
Rodney's slick coat, then slips through the blowing grasses
for miles. Watching muscle move under fine hair, I am riding with
Alexander on the Persian campaign. Trained and worked, men and
horses move together through lands they only imagined.

Trotting the hour lulls me past the day's soldier persona,
past sun-time and ego, to a day a thousand years ago
when I was a brave riding bareback, carrying a spear
fringed with dyed strips of buffalo hide, blessings
for hunting and battle. Once I was that native born warrior
watching muscle under shoulder ripple sunlight
from the horse's slick coat. Lift me up, straighten me
in the saddle, we have a long way to go.

NL

June 21st:

Lieutenant Blatz was emphasizing the necessity of doing something and not remaining inert when in command of troops in action.

War is kind-a like gambling, he said in his slow way, *and money won't grow in your hand.*

This is the way it is did. explains Reserve Captain Reno, late traffic policeman in Denver, and retaining all the language and mannerisms of the force. In appearance and action he resembles nothing so much as a cheap saloon-keeper. Truly we are to have a democratic army!

This is a time when *the last shall be first.* Men who have served an enlistment or two in the Regular Army, policemen, firemen—the type of men whose arms are tattooed, come into the limelight for a time and are subordinate officers who train the men in camps such as this one. Perhaps one man in twenty here is well-bred and has something of an education; then perhaps ten of the remaining nineteen have had some training at Kansas or Missouri University or similar institutions. But these sleep in their underwear, bathe only occasionally and insist upon using *guy* when they mean *man.*

However, I presume that a knowledge of the amenities is not needed to make efficient officers. At West Point, the idea was, they should be *officers and gentlemen.* But after all why need the new leaders know anything about forks? It's bayonets they need to know.

JOHN MASON

THE SENSES

I wander in the unchartered country of the Muses—none
Before me has set foot here—and I thrill to come upon
Springs untouched by any lips, and here to slake my thirst.
I joy to pluck strange flowers for a glorious wreath, the first
Whose brow the Muses ever crowned with blossoms from this
spot.
Why? Because I teach great truths, and set out to unknot
The mind from tight strictures of religion, and since I write
Of so darkling a subject in a poetry so bright,
Tingeing with the Muse's grace all subjects that I touch.

LUCRETIUS
Translated by A. E. Stallings

DUST

Wash the dust from my eyes, out of my ears,
from all pores where the wind has lodged it.
Wash it away—whatever is left from dusty roads
of childhood Rockport, dust of dead parents.
Let me go to Mess Hall clean,
to feed as well as my horse
for tomorrow's ride.
Break this monotony with abundant splashing
from fountains in Renaissance Rome.
Break this dead dusty road. I am going somewhere
lined with apple trees and red rose bushes.

NL

Aviation is calling the hot-blooded youth of our troop, now that it begins to seem that we may never get mounts.

Horace Wells, a clear-eyed, splendid type from Denver, passed the exams for it yesterday and leaves within a week for the University of Illinois where the training ground is. He has a wonderful and well-trained voice and hopes to study music professionally—when the war is over.

25 is the aviation limit, but physically perfect men are so rare that they will probably extend the limit. If they do, I think that many of us will have a try at it, since they have eliminated cavalry raids and cross-country riding from war.

July 1ˢᵗ:

A lad in the squad room, soft-cheeked and fresh from college, exposed his dreams of greatness by talking in his sleep the other night. Truly a Napoleonic conception was revealed.

Allied Armies, attention! he shouted.

As the story is re-told, he shouted:

General Joffre—right guide! General Haig—left guide! Generals, kings, and emperors,—front and center! King George, why haven't you polished your crown! etc. Albert, that is a filthy sceptre! Prisoners, attention! Wilhelm detailed to mow Lieutenant Smith's lawn!

The dwellers in the third floor squad room were coming painfully and with much complaint down the stairs to fall in for *Retreat*. Rifle butts clumping on the stairs, heads hanging and tiredness written all over their faces. *I believe I will come along,* shouted a jocose youth from the head of the stair dragging his rifle after him. *Do!* answered a dispirited voice. *I assure you that you won't intrude.*

July 28th:

A birthday that I had already borrowed from the future, and so passed without notice.

August 1st:

The past month has been one of intensive effort. During this month the possibilities of the men have become evident. From businessmen, professional men, farmers and clerks, they have traveled in this brief time a long way upon the road to soldierdom. Technically they're impossible but most of them are capable of directing a group of men to accomplish a desired result.

Even thus far only it has been the greatest experience in their lives, and if they pull through it will be long stamped upon their memory.

July's heat has been almost intolerable but we have drilled constantly and furiously. The men are all thin-faced and trained to the last minute. A little respite, a little change of program, alone can prevent their *going stale.*

August 29th, 1917:

Back to the Army again.

September 3rd, 1917:

Camp Funston:

A city of wood sprung up overnight where four months ago I had ridden in solitude miles from human habitation. 10,000 carpenters at work, trains puffing on scores of tracks, wagons, trucks and men scurrying here to there!

I find the officers of the former *First Troop* quartered together in barracks in Unit 312. I unfold my cot and bedding, open my army trunk, get out my mess kit and am again at home.

Colonel Crimmins' classes in modern warfare take up most of our time. Upon several occasions, the doughty Colonel forgets modern warfare and indulges in long personal narratives about his experiences in the Philippines or in Mexico.

One of the books read to us contains the following sage observation (written before 1914): *modern wars will be fought with small use of artillery and very mobile troops … they will be of brief duration, perhaps as short as six days.*

2nd Lieutenant Harold Beaton has a bunk next to me and resumes his studies on the 'eucalalie' where he left off Aug. 15th in our old 4th squad room after a summer's laborious effort. Harold can out-run, out-swim or out-fight any of the troop—but his musical ability is slight.

JOHN MASON

PREPARING FOR WAR

Day in, day out, we prepare our horses for battle,
brush their warm, shiny coats; train mules to pull
the gray metal field artillery.
Riding out across the prairie, we camp days out from barracks.
Caissons drawn by mule teams line the sky.
Their creaking competes with meadowlarks singing.

The young man rides, imagining himself the hero.
He has never heard the fire-power,
seen the barbed wire looming,
he has never heard the cries of wounded in shell holes.
Without the burning flames here on the plains
he gallops into the wind without the body
and the spirit blows away.

NL

THE NATURE OF THINGS

Now I'll explain how we can walk when we decide to go,
And how it's in our power to ply our members to and fro,
And by what process we are habitually able to convey
The body's heavy freight. So listen close to what I say:
I tell you, first, an *image* of walking comes into the mind,
And strikes it, as I've said before. Desire follows. You'll find
That no one starts to undertake a single act until
The mind has looked ahead and has decided that it will.
(What thing the mind foresees, there is an image of.)
And therefore when the mind rouses itself and wants to move
And walk, it stirs the whole force of the spirit scattered through
The limbs, all in a trice. And it's an easy thing to do,
Seeing that spirit and the mind so closely intermesh.
And spirit in turn prods the body, so all the mass of flesh
Is pushed ahead and moved little by little. Then, besides,
The body becomes more porous, and the air thus comes inside
(Naturally enough—it is so mobile), through the wide-
Opening passageways, abundantly, dispersing all
Throughout the body, down to every part, however small.
Therefore the body's borne along two different ways, by twinned
Forces, as a ship is borne along by sail and wind.

LUCRETIUS
Translated by A. E. Stallings

GEORGE RODNEY ON SUNDAY

I walk to the stable to saddle George Rodney. In his stall,
in the long stable row, his head is down. He is eating his noon hay.
Hearing me, he snuffles, and blows, shakes his head.
I open the stall door, he reaches out his nose to me.
I lift his neck in the crook of my elbow,
the warm weight of his neck pulls down.
Slipping the halter around his head,
I buckle it and snap on the shank. All the horses' heads
follow George Rodney and me as we walk the aisle to the tack room.
Bridle, martingale, saddle pad, saddle, girth, and tighten.
Nothing more, no saddle bags, no lance, no rifle, no bayonet.
I am taking George Rodney out for a Sunday ride.
We need a world view, a far horizon.

NL

September 13th:

As usual everything is *simulated*. We simulate guns, simulate troops, simulate night, until it becomes again the childhood game of *Let's play like …*

Received orders assigning me to command 41st Company and also designating me as *Acting in Command of 11th Battalion 164th Depot Brigade.*

September 14th:

We move from barracks to Officers' Quarters and begin to live more comfortably.

Wagered with Bill Barnett as follows:

1st : I wager $50 that war is over by or before March 1st, 1919
2nd: I wager $10 that war is over by September 14th, 1918.
Bill owes me $5.00 on previous wager.

September 15th:

I make my first morning reports.

Until the artillery quarters are finished we room with men in the 9th Battalion so Artillery may use our quarters. I am with Roy Van Bibber of Troy, Kansas. Roy is a delightful Missourian of the pure Missouri type, generous, hospitable, good-humored, disdainful of *Yanks* in general and more than fond of their society in particular case. He loves the thought that he is in the war game since it's going on—but when it's over he has ambitions to return to the country and raise jumping horses.

September 19th:

Depot Brigade draws some few hundred men. The troop trains pull up and disgorge their loads of prospective cannon sausage. Each county quota has a man of some intelligence in charge and he checks his party. They are grouped into aisles in a long shed: Missourians together, Nebraskans grouped, etc.

Instead of the state abbreviations above, some veteran of the Training Camp at Riley urged a sign: *Ye who enter here leave hope behind.*

The Arizona contingent is made up most frequently of lean-faced cow-punchers who hobble instead of walk and wear quilted boots and wide beaver sombreros. One deputation from that state had a lone Chinaman following placidly along. Poor John—he did seem lonesome.

Nebraska sends husky Swedes with lantern jaws and dull eyes. High-handed, stiff-shouldered men who can lift great weights but cannot think rapidly. They ask for 44 undershirts and size 11½ shoes, and 6⅞ hats.

Kansas sends clean, decent looking people with evidence of education and intelligence. Really a superior lot.

JOHN MASON

INFORMATION

At Rockport I ran to beat the boys
down the steep hill to meet the steamboat.
The calliope piped its coming with songs like
Oh! Susannah. News arrived with the men in suits and hats
on the steamboat. *What's happening in the world?*
our townsmen asked. We boys listened.

Tall yellow flowers, ironweed and thistle waved along the shore.
What goes in Washington in this new millennium?
Are people settling along the river? I wanted to know.
The price of tobacco affected our family warehouse.

The war story goes that the generals miss the mark
because they don't know. The runners get lost, or get captured.
Armies mire in the quicksand for lack of information.
I will find out first, to save our troops.

NL

WHAT RETURN FOR THIS WAR

I am thinking glory is a paltry pennant for all this work
and fear. These men in training starve for food and tenderness.
I hear supplies don't make it to the troops. They die from lack
of ammunition, much less food, sugar, weapons, shelter.
The worst was Gallipoli when soldiers drowned in their trenches,
then froze in place. Quarter of a million troops, their bodies still
upright.

We train on dry land here in Kansas, retire to warm barracks,
are served hot rations. Horses are tended, mules, too.
How would we guess that mud drowns caissons, and the rest?
There are limits to imagining.

NL

THE HOUND

She left the way she came, one cold day,
her long ears trailing, white-tipped flag waving,
following scent on the ground.
Was she drowned, pulled apart in a coyote fight?
Deep as mid-stream river, this flowing sadness.
She may be hunting nearby on a wooded slope.
I hope she comes home.

NL

Missouri sends all kinds: wild men from the Ozarks, *club men* from Saint Louis, farmers from the northern part of the state and miners from Joplin. On the whole they are not much of an average. One came in from Calloway County carrying a shotgun ready to do his part. He is the first unbattled farmer I have seen. Another from the same county forgot what state he was from and knew practically nothing of any other states or countries.

Southern Colorado and New Mexico were largely Mexican, and a tougher bunch of brigands I have seldom seen.

Captain Coffin has about 60% Mexicans who cannot understand the commands. They are all small in stature so the tall half of the company is white, and the other half is short and bends over to see what the first half has done when an order is given.

September 29th:

Lieutenant Perryman (12th Brigade), Chillecothe, Missouri, tested his platoon on the correct transmission of orders. To the right flank man he whispered: *Enemy is in sight on height above Division Headquarters; reported to be a battalion; take a squad and tell me upon return how many men behind the hill.*

The message traveled down the line of recruits, reached four Mexicans who took it seriously and viewed the indicated hill in great alarm and consternation, in their excitement garbling the message more than ever. When the last man repeated the message to the Lieutenant, it was simply this, *How many men are in Hell?*

What strange bedfellows war throws together! It is truly a great game in many ways despite its nauseating qualities.

1st Lieutenant Daniel J. McCarthy (ex Irish army Sergeant) has 2nd Lieutenant McIntosh, a Creek Indian with his outfit, and the recruits are all Swedes. When *Dan'l* read *Kelly* in the roster he called for that individual at once; *Let me see that Kelly,* he asked. Kelly proved to have lost all Irish qualities and was the meekest Swede in the Co. much to *Dan'l's* discomfiture.

Captain Ted White (30th Company) drew a morphine fiend to whom he administers a regular supply of dope and also a pacifist who refuses to drill or to wear a uniform. As Colonel Hawkins said, *The man seems to have no objection towards government food though.*

Colonel Hawkins (Colonel 2nd Training Unit 164th Depot Brigade) is a born soldier, son of a soldier, graduate of St. Cyr (French Cavalry School) and as gentle and kindly a man as we ever meet. He looks every inch a cavalryman, speaks longingly of the hoped for orders that will mount us, and means too that cavalry is not a dead arm of the Service.

JOHN MASON

COUNTER TO DARKNESS

It isn't my nature to hate the haters.
That drought curls leaves.
Encouraging lost men to ride
athletic horses—more like it.

NL

EARLY MESS

I did not choose this war. I'm not sure the chiefs did either.
Strange feeling early in the day, pre-dawn breakfast.
Bismarck's siege of Paris starved the people, slowly,
until one day they ate rats, and raged at each other,
killing neighbors. Our genetic drive to war defeats us.

I try not to act as I feel, but as I think. These poor blokes
take orders like horses take the spur. They don't read.
I go as cup-bearer, boot-polisher, commander of beans.
As a server, I remember Lucretius,
In actuality, it is not possible to find
In every single body an intelligence and mind.

NL

TWO MULES NAMED SARGEANT AND CORPORAL

The late Roy White of Manchester was a First Lieutenant during World War I. One of his duties was as censor of letters written by the soldiers to the folks back home. One letter he read went something like this:

Dear Pa,

When I get out of this here army I'm coming home and buy me the meanest two mules I can find. I will name one of them Sargeant and the other Corporal and then I'm going to spend the rest of their lives cussin' and beating them.

Your loving son,

Bill

JESS WILSON

TARGET RANGE LINGO

September 19th:

Off early in the morning with *light packs* (containing mess kit only) across the parade ground, around the officers' homes, past the flag pole at the cavalry post and west past the stone-walled cemetery, on past the shaded grove with its scores of little jumps then out by the *Pump House* and the polo field until in the distance a large red flag is seen fluttering from a stubby pole.

The *pit detail* is marched back to the long row of targets that extends along the base of the hill, and they disappear into the pits, or *butts*, where for hours bullets whine and hum just overhead, and ricochets with their dust and pebbles scattered down into the pit.

JOHN MASON

A WALK BEYOND THE BASE

Walking out beyond the base without my shirt
I receive October sun the way the amber prairie
takes it in. Hazel and orange, green and yellow,
grasses blow against the huge sky. I raise my arms
up and down like a raptor rising to thermals.
Would that I could soar above war this way.
My appetite for vast land exceeds desire for food.
Beauty in any form makes me delirious.
Breath of wind in grasses is my breath.
Sun between my shoulder blades, my strength.

NL

HOW IT IS OVER THERE WITH EUROPEAN CAVALRY
The Need for a Smith

The telltale clink of a loose nail warned a cavalryman that he must find the shoeing smith if he were to keep up next day with the column; the same sound to the senior driver of a gun-team threatened the mobility of his six harnessed animals. There were five thousand horses in an infantry division in 1914, more than five thousand in a cavalry division. All had to be kept shod and healthy if the twenty miles of the day were to be covered to timetable, the infantry fed, reconnaissance reports returned, small arms combat fire covered by artillery fire should the enemy be encountered. Fourteen miles of road was filled by an infantry division on the march and the endurance of horses—those pulling the wheeled field kitchens, cooking on the march, quite as much as those drawing the ammunition wagons of the artillery brigades—counted with that of the infantry in the race to drive the advance forward.

JOHN KEEGAN

THE ONES WHO FOUGHT

Sikh cavalry rode into smoke and firing guns, but what
gave them sorrow was winter, the freezing of limbs,
lack of fodder for their mounts. They reported
to British command, their occupying force in India.

The French brought in their colonials, such as Zouaves,
Algerian troops in red pantaloons and black jackets
trimmed in red, with red head-covers.
French officers wore red and blue, Senegalese, khaki.

British kept to khaki: the oil cloth over wool,
a week of near-freezing rain, then snow,
wind to freeze the ears off, all night without heat,
wet boots, frozen feet. The wall of the trench
held by rotting boards and men.

Plans do not determine outcomes.
Who had counted on the weight of gear?
The foot soldier of every country carried a ten-pound
rifle, 100 rounds, a bayonet, water bottle, a pack
with dry socks and shirt, rations and field dressing,
at least sixty pounds, for twenty miles a day.

Horses endured crossed messages between generals.
Attack would turn to retreat, up and back, forty miles.
Men and beasts became the same, exhausted beings.

NL

ANTICIPATION OF THE TRENCHES

I was going to France on a horse,
I would carry a lance, and ride him very fast.
But things expected will not happen—
more undone than love gone one-sided.
War is a drudge without horses.
Mounts trained for war will stay in Kansas.

NL

October 4th, 1917
2:30 a.m.:

148 Missourians arrive. I assign them to the 44th Co. We wait until dawn to run them through the cold showers. Several are drunk, but do not long continue so after the cold water strikes them.

The Battalion begins to fill up. My own Company the 41st, has 166 men by night: clean Kansas farmers from Marshall, Washington, Hemcha, and Seneca counties; cow-punchers in boots and wearing wide sombreros come in from Union County, New Mexico. In this latter group of 46 there are about 15 Mexicans, some are shriveled warty little rats, others bright-eyed with an oriental cleanness and appearance.

The First Sergeant Geiser transferred from the Regular Army home address, Owensboro, Kentucky, proves to be an excellent man at handling recruits.

My 2nd Lieutenant Euett Williams, formerly with the First Troop at the 84th P.T.R. at Fort Riley, is a quick, industrious intelligent youngster of fine character and sturdy strength. He is very friendly with the men and much liked.

2nd Lieutenant Castlen should be a Captain: an excellent chap, well-bred, well-educated, clean-cut and full of nerve and *hoss sense.*

The Company work goes off very smoothly, the new are anxious and willing to learn, the officers capable and reliant.

JOHN MASON

October 11th:

I appointed the following non-coms:

1st Sergeant:	Sergeant Geiser
Sergeants:	Caywood, traveling salesman
Supply:	Cyrus S. Duffy Webber
Bruce Malery:	*Con man*
Maneval:	Undertaker
Corporals:	Lealdes Earhart: telegraph and clerk
Joseph Spielman:	Farmer
Fay Newton	
Rudolf Edlkraut	
Priest	
Mess:	Recruit Harris

October 11th:

Orders came to the effect that we will transfer our white troops to southern camps and receive 14,000 negroes in their places. Much dejection among the officers of the 11th Battalion all of whom had become attached to their commands and want to fight through the war with them.

JOHN MASON

Building at Fort Riley

Friend on a wooden horse

**Polo field at
Fort Riley**

The camp

STORM ON THE PRAIRIE IN KANSAS

So widely does the huge supply of space unfold
With no borders, out in all directions.
Nature won't permit the sum of things to ring
Itself with any kind of limit.

—Lucretius (Translated by A. E. Stallings)

Black perspective, deep in front, sweeping to the horizon's
burnt umber sky over the rust gold prairie grass, as far
as you can see. Forlorn is a tree out there. I wonder when the
storm will hit us. The funnel is spinning its top to suck up
all things earth, whirling up ribbons, rabbits, wolves,
babies, houses, trees, all things of atoms, swerving, re-forming.
It makes such a roar. A long war, telescoped. Things once loved,
hammered to forgetfulness, back to wind.
Bring me water in a bowl. I will offer it to the Great Mother.

NL

October 13th:

Lieutenant Daniel J. McCarthy insists tonight at mess that the Negro troops are only *lampblacked Irishmen.*

The ½ Training Unit (under command of Colonel Ralph McCoy U.S.A.) is ordered to march a couple of miles up into the hills for an address by the Commanding Officer 89th Division, General Leonard Wood. As next in rank to Colonel McCoy, I march the three Battalions (2500 men) up and form them in a small depression on the table-land. Gen. Wood, stout, nervously energetic, gallops up, dismounts, limps (he has a bad leg) into place and predicts a long and fierce war ahead for us.

It is a great game—this preparation for the Great Adventure. Most of us are really tremendously interested in it, and vain of our boots and spurs and power. A few months from now some of us won't be so fond of it I'll warrant—yet the thrill of *taking a chance* will add spice to life.

13 Lt. Daniel J. McCarthy insists
tonight at mess that the
negro troops are only "camp blacked
Irishmen."

13 We discover a Denver Country
Club Chef in the draft & prepare
to start the 11th Bn. Mess.

It is a great game – this preparation
for the Great Adventure. Most of
us are really tremendously interested
in it & vain of our boots & spurs
& power. A few months from
now some of us won't be so fond
of it I'll warrant — yet the
thrill of "taking a chance" will
add spice to life.

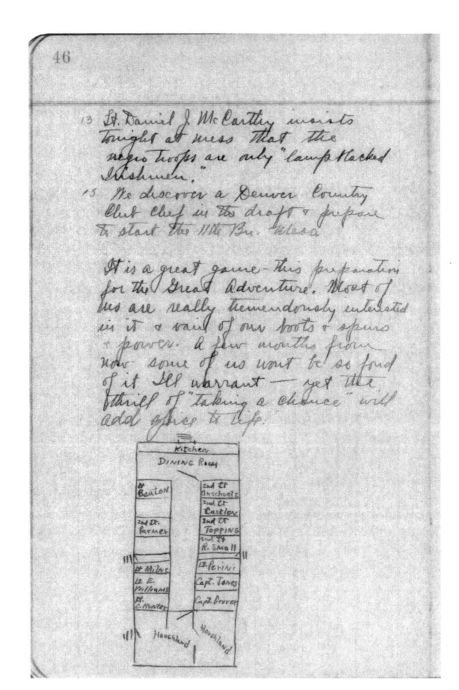

**John Mason draws a sketch of the Mess table
with himself as head of Mess**

November 13th:

The Battalion approached the 900 mark and then is depleted by successive transfers to Camp Kearney California, Camp Pike, Arkansas, Camp Doriphon, Oklahoma, to fill up National Guard Divisions. My new Mexicans in Company 41 went to Camp Kearney, California. An hour before they left I found the appended note upon my desk in a large box of excellent cigars. I was never more surprised, for I rather imagined that men in my command did not like me—since I worked them so much harder and exacted so much stricter discipline than surrounding commanders.

Daniel J. McCarthy (ex First Sergeant) says *When a man has been through the Cooks and Bakers School and returns to his troop they generally put him in the blacksmiths' shop.*

Dan'l's cryptic observations reflect the opinion of most reserve officers upon Army business methods.

All Cavalry Officers National Army ordered recommissioned in either Artillery or Infantry in accordance with General Staff's plan not to attempt any use of cavalry in this war.

I was recommissioned and made a Captain of Field Artillery.

<u>Captain.</u>

JOHN MASON

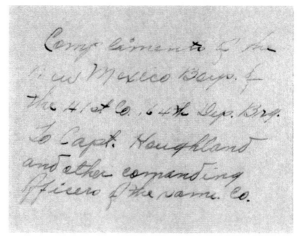

READING LUCRETIUS

It's sweet to know from what misfortunes you are free.

—Lucretius (Translated by A. E. Stallings)

Reading Lucretius, I ache to think I am alone in this flat land,
my life determined by military hierarchy. Where I am stationed,
which horse I ride. They decide my fate, although fate is mine.
Not even they know what country calls me. Wind blows dust
to blind my vision. I trust my horse will know the way.
After all, maybe not to France this time.
The West wind is free and freshens.
New things are formed in empty space. Dust, alive, accretes.

NL

BECOMING ONE

The universe is harmonic or it wouldn't work. Heraclitus announced almost three thousand years ago that the harmony of the universe, that is, of everything, is hidden.

—Guy Davenport

How long will it take for leaves blown loose
to merge with soil, for dogwood to offer
four-fold petals to the spring's blue sky?

NL

WIND

She forces her way over the plain lifting water from the grasses.
Deer and horses have retreated from her fleet pursuit.
They hide in the creek bed copses, huddled in Blue Stem.
She sees the hiding places and pelts them with rain.

NL

1918

1st Lieutenant Jack White Brown of Tacoma, Washington, *beau saveur,* horseman, bronco buster, polo player, sportsman,—*a gentleman unafraid* reports and is assigned to "C" Troop. A veteran of the Spanish American War, one of those delightful, well-bred souls, destined to be in any wars or excitement that came up, and to carry their part through with ease and dash.

JOHN MASON

February 26, 1918

Uncle Dick Holmes writes that he knows *God can conjure me back* safely from the war, and if not we will meet *in the circil beyond the Sun.*

Lieutenant Auerman, than whom there is no more continuous conversationalist, confides in me that he has discovered that the way to flatter people is to listen to them. He proves himself no sycophant.

March 8th:

At the 342nd Officers' Club, Colonel Nugent told of the telegram General Hunter sent his Commanding Officer upon one occasion in the P.I. when he as a Major was organizing a new Squadron of Cavalry. The Gen. as I knew him a few months ago was an old school cavalryman of the irritable type who damned everybody under him for everything they did. The telegram:

> *I have three hundred men who have never seen a horse: three hundred horses that have never seen a man—and fifteen officers who have never seen either.*

Colonel Nugent also told the story of the Irishman who wandered into a bar-room where a fistie altercation was being engaged in by a number of well-dressed men. Watching for a time, he edged closer and closer, then cleared his throat and spoke: *Excuse me gentlemen, is this a private fight —or can anybody get in?*

Jack Lehman, (St. Louis) the Regimental Adjutant then told of a speech his father made to an Hibernian meeting in St. Louis about the time of the Boer War.

Gentlemen, wherever in the world there is a battle for the sweet name of Freedom you will find Irishmen in the front line—of both sides.

March 27th:

Division Review north of Morris hill by General Wrin. I realized with joy that the horse is still a factor in war. Never so many together before. The two Artillery regiments (540th and 341st) went by with some 1300 horses each; then the ammunition train with 5 or 6 hundred; then the pack trains with their long lines of pack mules and the supply trains with larger and less patient long-eared hybrids; the engineers, the medical corps, all mounted. But in all that melee of mounts there was none for me! *Oscar Blair* indeed!

Coming home one of the Ozark Missourians in "A" Battery started singing:

When the Roll is called up yonder I'll be there.

You may be, rudely interrupted Sgt. Abernathy, *you shore ain't never been present when hit's called down here.*

March 29th:

We receive 36 recruits. What poor hollow-chested weaklings they seem in comparison with our veterans of six months intensive drill. Already the men seem inclined to swagger and strut and pose as seasoned campaigners. The recruits eye them enviously—these men who know how to handle a rifle and when to salute.

JOHN MASON

ON MORTALITY AND THE SOUL

For what's this great and wicked lust for living all about,
If it just drives us to distraction, amidst danger and doubt?
The life of mortals has a limit set to it, my friend.
Death has no loopholes. All of us must meet it in the end.
We go through the same motions in the same old place.
    No measure
Of added life will ever coin for us a novel pleasure.
True, while we lack that which we long for, it is an obsession,
But we will just crave something *else* once it's in our possession;
We are forever panting with an unquenched thirst for life.
No one knows what the years to come will bring—what
    joy or strife
May lie in store for us, what outcome's looming in our lot.
But by adding on to life, we don't diminish by one jot
The length of death, nor are we able to subtract instead
Anything to abbreviate the time that we are dead.

Though you outlive as many generations as you will,
Nevertheless, Eternal Death is waiting for you still.
It is no shorter, that eternity that lies in store
For the man who with the setting sun *today* will rise no more,
Than for the man whose sun has set months, even years, before.

LUCRETIUS
Translated by A. E. Stallings

IN FACE OF DEATH

In face of death I walk the fields against the sun.
Green grass lies beneath the straw.
Oaks lean away from the west wind
as if they would not be pushed
towards their westward destiny.
A herd of black steers watches from the gate.
Curious, they stand together as one.
Great Mother, we all face it.

NL

LOST, A FRIEND WHO DIED IN WAR

Ravens feed in the last green grass before winter.
When hope looks up to possibility, Juliet sings to Romeo,
exquisite notes against the gale.
The empty chair rocks in the wind,
reminding me it's empty.

If I had a beloved woman near at dawn
we would watch sienna grasses blow,
talk about the beauty of the prairie as if it were the sea
and we were sitting on the pier.

NL

WORD COMES FROM ACROSS THE SEA

Who could persuade us to give up the filigreed sword?
Bred in fire, pulled from stone by brave warriors?
The English won't hear of it, in spite of rapid fire machine guns.
General Haig won't go near the trenches where he sends in boys.
He says it might demoralize him, so he parades with pennants,
then lunches on quail and *foie gras*. He commands Lance corporals
to sustain the name and carry lances, long and unwieldy as they are.
Milner and French, generals from the Boer War, swore on their swords
the Cavalry would bring victory to England. Their mistresses came to
drink champagne, crystal raised to glory. That week they lost thousands.

NL

The cavalry, once so shiny in polished boots and bright uniforms, now stained and muddy, sway in their saddles, dazed with fatigue. *The men's heads hang with weariness,* writes an officer of Hussars with the 9th Cavalry Division. *They only half see where they are going; they live as in a dream. At halts the famished and broken-down horses even before unsaddling, plunge at the hay and devour it voraciously. We no longer sleep; we march by night and face the enemy by day.*

BARBARA TUCHMAN

CAMP FUNSTON

Camp Funston was located on the Fort Riley military reservation near Junction City, Kansas. The facility, named after Brigadier General Frederick Funston, was the largest of 16 divisional cantonment training camps built during World War I to house and train soldiers for military duty. Construction began in July 1917 and buildings were laid out uniformly in city block squares with main streets and side streets on either side. An estimated 2,800 to 4,000 buildings were constructed at the camp to accommodate more than 40,000 soldiers from the U.S. Army's 89th Division, who were stationed at the facility. The camp cost roughly $10 million to build.

The camp resembled more a city than an army camp. Besides containing housing and training centers, the camp offered general stores, theaters, social centers, infirmaries, libraries, schools, workshops, and a coffee-roasting house. The sleeping barracks were 43 feet by 140 feet and two stories high. In them were a kitchen, mess hall, company commander's office, supply rooms, and squad rooms or dormitories. There were 150 beds in each sleeping room, as that was the size of an infantry company in 1917.

Funston's main purpose was to train soldiers drafted in midwestern states to fight overseas. Men would spend their hours drilling and learning new military techniques that became popular within World War I. Many officers were brought in from other countries such as France and Britain to train the Midwest soldiers. In their free time soldiers could see a show at the theaters or visit one of the social centers. However, many spent their time writing letters home. James H. Dickson, who served in the 356th Infantry Regiment of the 89th Division, wrote this to friends back home: *Eunice don't be to [sic] long about writing for news is scarce out in Kansas the wind blows it all away.*

Another soldier, Otto Bruner, wrote of a concert he saw while at Funston: *Last Thursday night I went to hear a big orchestra from St. Louis there were about eighty in it, it was fine. I also heard Madam Schumann-Heinke sing. I sure like to hear her sing. I don't know whether I spelt her name right or not but guess you will know who I mean.*

One of the biggest problems faced within the camp was the spread of communicable disease. Although all soldiers were inoculated upon entering the camp, the 1918–1920 influenza pandemic was said to have started within Camp Funston. Soldiers thought to have any communicable disease were immediately quarantined until they either got over the disease or were thought free of it.

After the war Camp Funston became a *mustering-out* center as soldiers prepared to return to civilian life. In 1924 the military decommissioned the 2,000 acre site with the dismantling of the buildings. Today a few foundations remain of the camp and a stone obelisk in honor of *The Men Who Trained at Funston for the Great War.*

KANSAS STATE HISTORICAL SOCIETY
(www. kshs.org)

LA BASSÉE, THE ROYAL WELCH

Waiting for the big advance, the troops hold
for the lucky shot of rum always passed before attack.
Soldiers wait in the rain to go over, on command.
The rum man runs up, retching, in the rain,
falls down in the mud, spills the most of three gallons—
all but what he had drunk himself. The Sergeant's
boot pushes his head into the mud, and stands on it.

We throw the whistling cylinders out to No Man's Land.
Distorted air, vapors hover like fog, blow back
into our trenches, filling them yellow.
Flimsy gas masks, supplied to soldiers,
made us look like Mars men,
gaps at the temple let in the gas.

It happens at La Bassée. Just as we are going over
the top of the trenches to fight, we inhale.
Company A attacks without the lucky rum.

The Germans put on efficient masks, shoot
the gas cylinders in our trenches. They emit, explode.
We run, run into German wire too strong for our guns to shoot down.
Caught, we are targets for machine guns, and
in the end, breathing in was our fatal mistake.

NL

DEAD BONES

Both on dry land and on the deep
Make the mad machinery of war drift off to sleep
For only you can favor mortal men with peace.

—Lucretius (Translated by A. E. Stallings)

Dead bones of horses buried under fire.

Their ashes blow in March wind.

Young men die before their children are born.

NL

IT WASN'T ALLOWED

We couldn't speak of the unspeakable.
The government censored our postcards—
the only line remaining on the postal form was,
I am quite well. When John was shot, he fell
in pieces. We couldn't pick him up under the barrage.
He was one of many. They lay out there in the blackened mud.
I didn't say anything about the crusted diarrhea,
the raspy breathing, bronchitis from nights out
standing watch in the trench in cold wind, and wet.
A long time without feeling feet—like moving stumps.
The only way to feel what others feel is to be one of them.
None of us is well. None of us expects to be well.
We are lost in the roar and crack, the loudness of this war.

NL

DANGEROUS TO LOSE THE STORY

When the story is lost, we are innocent of memory
then sacrifice all over again,
depriving the future of possibility—
withholding open fields from children's dreams.

I am a live intelligence.
Will I be when I am mud, mud, and so cold, cold?
One war after another. So little space for peace.

NL

December 19, 1917

The holidays approaching and with them a lonesome feeling, a desire to be for a time with old friends. Tonight I sat in my stall—the little pine-walled room is only that—and grew restless. The mathematics of artillery repelled my thoughts, the naïve dribble of the lieutenants in adjoining rooms, as usual, bored me. And I picked up old Marcus Aurelius, the greatest philosopher and man of a thousand years. I thought of him *among the Quadi* at the head of his army standing off the inroad of barbarians and at night in his tent weighing and balancing life.

> *In man's life time is but a moment; being a flux; sense is dim; the material frame corruptible; soul an eddy of breath; fortune a thing inscrutable; and fame precarious ... life a warfare and a sojourning; and after fame oblivious. What then can direct our goings? One thing and one alone, philosophy.*
>
> *Is the emerald less perfect for lacking praise?*

MARCUS AURELIUS

To accept life as it is,—what a creed! The only creed I believe.

JOHN MASON

December 24th:

Only 5% of the men allowed Xmas passes. The most terrible epidemic of misfortune occurred in families of the 95% left: a deluge of wires. *Sally very sick,—come home at once.*

Christmas Eve:

The Battery celebrates in … a smoker. *Square dancing* proves to be the popular feature of the evening, the boxing matches, an apple eating contest; jigging, singing, black face comedians, etc. contribute to the fun. Cider, pop-corn, apples, and candy are the refreshments. Everybody hurrahed and had an uproarious time.

December 28th:

Last night a dance in Junction City. After months of the monotony of Camp, the atmosphere of soft lights, music and white shoulders was indeed a delight. Van Bibber and I went in and took Martha Roark and her sister, Mrs. Lambert. In any town (excepting some Okla. towns) there are always human beings. Generally they prove to be of Celtic descent. How they flash the humor and the joy of living! The search ended. Funny and wonderful game—this life. Van and I stayed at the Bartell House and had a desperate time extricating ourselves from our boots, without the friendly assistance of a boot-jack.

JOHN MASON

CHRISTMAS, BARRACKS

Merry, merry, men in barracks.
Some going home to wives and babies.
Merriment's horn does not call to me.
I hear only TAPS. Europe endures a war
every generation. Our Civil War hardly finished,
we are in the trenches, lances against guns.
What was my calling here to this flat land?
Wind called, endless howling wind.
Polish my boots, clean the spurs, tomorrow
we ride out early.

NL

December 30th:

That Old Hindoo Proverb

> *Four things greater than all things are,*
> *Women and horse, power and war.*

How that old Hindoo proverb hits the nail on the head. Van Bibber, Mrs. (Sara) Lambert and I went to a "movie." As they generally prove to be, this one was an insult to any intelligence—but we had a delightful time anyhow. Mrs. L. is a star: clever but not too clever; pretty—but not concerned about it; sane, clear-eyed, and always watching the comedy of the game. She lives in that delightful old Kansas town of Emporia, is married to *a rising young lawyer,* and has a small son, age 15 months.

You live years before you find a man like Jack Cleary, a horse like *George Rodney,* or a woman like Mrs. L. The immortals to whom the Gods have given hearts.

January 1st:

The years that have slipped away before never made their adieus with such grace, nor whispered promise that the succeeding ones waited open-armed. But this one was a lovely sprite who told us good-bye and blew an elusive kiss across her finger-tips before the curtain hid her.

The new one—and perhaps for some of us the last one—stole softly into the mellow cadence of an old waltz and Lo! We held in our arms the wondrous sweetness, the mystery, and the promise of life!

The *Community House* was packed with soldiers and their sweethearts and the crowd whirled and ... and laughed and struggled in the intoxication of the dance. The room was a blur of drab uniforms, colored dresses, strange faces.

It's like a sea, she said softly, and at the words an old verse stole into my consciousness:

Thou wast that all to me Love
For which my soul did pine,
A green isle in the sea Love,
A fountain and a shrine.

Somewhere far across the waters waited the great adventure,—but there for us all was the greater adventure—Life.

JOHN MASON

Sara

Sara holds his horse

Horses in training

Sara in the field

January 2nd:

Perhaps at some disputed barricade,
When Spring comes back with rustling shade.

There shall be for a fleeting instant the highest note of joy.

But thus far in the journey the purest melody was this night.

A huge orange moon, a winding road, the filaments of frost upon the car windows,

—and Happiness.

Pure Happiness, the *Holy Grail* for which we ever seek—and might have never known.

JOHN MASON

SARA

The field is suddenly beset
by yellow butterflies rising,
swooping, joining in rapid flights
making active air.

Thoughts of you dominate
my green pasture—your blonde
curls, the yellow butterflies.
Their wings carry your song to me,
uplift your courtship to mine.

NL

AFTER THE FALL OF GREAT HOUSES

After the fall of ruling houses,
when lords lose servants, ballrooms are curtained,
I will go on my own to drill for oil.
A tough business, dirty, up in risky mountains, or
in the Panhandle. No one to blame but me for the
wrong site. One more dry well, one more character builder—
my words. I'll make the money for the family who follows.

One of us might build a brick house in Federal style,
glossy green door with a brass knocker,
brick path lined with boxwood—I can smell it
in the rain. A paneled entrance, old wood floors,
fine rugs, a tray of champagne to greet the guests.

Outside on river gravel, four shiny, harnessed horses
hitched to a carriage finished in black lacquer, lined in gabardine,
harness in patent leather, with polished brass lanterns and buckles.
Two men in black coats stand at the bridles, holding the horses
while the *whip* goes inside for a glass.
A lot to go back to—the daily use of four-in-hand for travel, and
time to drive a distance.
Some will shoot quail, some hunt the fox with tri-color hounds.
To retrieve these sports I plan to work.
That's what's different. It's not given by noble heritage.

Living well won't happen by singing in the wind.

NL

DREAM

Does fantasy come of a dying brain? Or a better mind?
When the beings gather, the ants and elephants,
is theirs a better dream than ours?

I'm gliding on the wind-chime breeze to a place
within the place, born of sun on my skin.
I know the stars live behind the clouds,
bright ones being born, while the dog dreams.

See the yellow butterfly about to fly south?
It's a long way to fly on a breeze. Yellow flecks
from its wings will join the cosmic dust. So will I.
Yellow flecks from inside my iris will join new stars
so they can see.

NL

January 13th:

This last thing known
He can court danger, laugh at perilous odds,
And, pillowed on a memory so sweet,
Meets oblivious eternity
Without regret yields his victorious soul,
The blessed pilgrim of a vow fulfilled.

Sunday night. A broiled chicken, delicious hot chocolate, strawberry preserves, I become a gourmand.

January 20th: Sunday

A snowy walk in the country with *Bud* barking at every passerby. That chorus from *The Road to Mandalay* I had waited three days to hear again:

Come ye back ye British soldier....

January 21st:

W.D. orders that all soldiers must stand Reveille. Such a swearing and sputtering and hurrying about. *The end of a perfect day*, said Lieutenant Auerman, *but the wrong end.*

January 24th:

Auerman again, *I had been in the Army four months, and learned a lot of things about blood and human nature.*

John Mason's sister, Janet:

Well I am glad if you have found the feminine equivalent to so vagrant a soul.

January 26th:

Sunday. An open fire rather than a *jug of wine beneath bough* furnishes all the contentment needed.

Announcement is made of the marriage, February 9, of Capt. John M. Hougland, formerly of Tulsa, Ok., and Miss Sara R. Lambert of Emporia, Kas., by the Rev. H. S. Church of this city. Captain Hougland is with his regiment at Camp Funston while Mrs. Hougland is living in Kansas City.

Sara, his dream

EPILOGUE

John Mason married Sara in 1918 and continued to train men for war, but he never was ordered to land in its fray in France.

Armistice was declared November 11, 1918. When John Mason was released from his duties as Captain, and free to live his life with Sara, they went in pursuit of oil from the Panhandle to the Colorado mountains, well into Wyoming's expanse. Sara packed them up for each move—fifty-five times.

John Mason was a risk-taker, an adventurer, who encountered a grizzly bear on a mountain path at night, with a knife as his only weapon. He came home wearing the skin.

In the course of his time in the West, he sought to learn the wisdom of Indian leaders about the Earth, the ways human-kind could live in harmony with Her. He had great respect for the ways of Native Americans, and taught me that understanding.

In Cody, Wyoming I entered the Irma Hotel. I saw the bar, polished by westerners' sleeves, and imagined his sitting there. I could feel his presence.

When John Mason and Sara decided to leave the constant wind and dust, they moved to Tennessee. They found and restored a house used as a hospital in the Civil War. He told his grandchildren about the headless horseman who rode into the living room to leave the bloodstains on the floor, still there.

Naming the place "Green Pastures," they intended for it to be their permanent home, which it was. It became a center of civility. Poets, leaders, horsemen, thinking people gathered there to discuss things in beautiful surroundings. Fabrics, furniture, and many books made the house a destination. Sara's warmth and John Mason's tales brought many people to their table.

His gas and oil company, "Spur" became well-known in the south. Each gas station had a garden around its Georgian brick building. Before he died, John Mason sold it to Murphy Oil in 1959.

John Mason and Sara loved each other until the end, never had to go to war, inspired the grandchildren with a will to enter the world to help it along.

NANA LAMPTON

Appendix

It is a strangely beautiful thing—Mason to Sara

Tuesday night
12/6/18

Sara—

It is a strangely beautiful thing—
this finding the one of whom you have
dreamed and finally despaired. To awake
and know that you are on earth is
to face each new day with happiness.
What matters the yearning that is almost
pain, the longing that almost defies
every reasonable conclusion and whispers
"go to her ... be near her .... nothing else
matters." One must walk in the shadow
to appreciate the light. And the shadow
is only intolerable when one believes
that there is no light. Knowing that
the sunlight finds the road a little
way ahead is almost in itself a
compensation.

When I realize, as I do many times
a day, that you _are_ — I thrill with
startled delight. "A thrill chaser" I

too may be. If so I have accomplished
everything, for I have the secret to
unending thrills. I have but to remember
the wonderous gentleness of your heart,
the pure beauty of your thought, the
innate fineness of your soul, and I
have the thrill. Now there is no thrill
so great as the one a neophyte knows
when he learns of a fineness of thought
above his most idealistic dream.
And you have that. A few words
you spoke to me in the stillness of
a night left me with such an awe
that I shall ever feel an inclination
to fling myself prostrate at your feet.
At times I tremble for fear that I
may be so unworthy, so gross a
soul that you will lose an infinite
portion of that spirit of beauty —
and then I know that there can

be but one result of our association:
I shall become the better for it. The
fineness of a heart like yours is
above and beyond danger from any
source.

Oh Sara, if I could but make you
know what you mean to me! I have
found all that I could ever imagine
groping for.

And then there is the thrill of
knowing that so fine a heart is
so beautifully enclosed. I am not
big enough to despise my senses,
nor shall ever be as long as life
is in me now. To suddenly remember
the beauty of you, the magic of your
eyes, the slim curves of your
body, the rioting sweetness of your
hair — and the soft sweet
madness of your lips, —— it is

enough to bring happiness were I
a soul doomed to eternal torment.
I would care more for you than
most men can even dream of
caring for the one woman, even if you
were selfish and heartless, for looking
into your eyes I could never even
imagine anything but a beauty of
spirit. And to know first that
beauty, and then to know the
beauty that is visible to any eyes
makes me forever grateful to the
Gods.

Tonight I have but one concern —
the memory of the hurt look that
crossed your face when I told you
that you had lived in so materialistic
an atmosphere that you expected
only an affection that demanded

security and a conservative percentage of return. I was so in earnest, so anxious that you come to understand that I loved you with all my heart forever and without change, that I purposely spoke roughly to shock you into a conviction. I fear that I only succeeded in wounding.

Some day you will know that nothing I might say or do could in the smallest way be intended to hurt you. I ask only that I may have the opportunity to prove to you that you mean more to me than myself, and that I would pay eternal sorrow as a price if it bought you happiness.

Should I ever need punishment for sin, the belief that I have

brought you one small bit of lasting
regret or hurt will torment me
as never man should be.

And none can have so great a
reward as I if I come at last to
the end of the lane and know
that the journey was happier to
you with me at your side than
it could have been otherwise.

Love you said could not stand still.
I thought it impossible to love you
more. But I do. I have but glimpsed
the love of you. It will take a lifetime—
gladness, sorrow, hardships and
success, or mayhap dire failure, for
me to even dimly comprehend the
different reasons why you should be
loved

Mason

RARE

A fabulous bird high in the tree
white breast towards the sun
one I've never seen before
pitching with the branch
in the wind. This feeling.

NL

ALMANAC

John Mason to Sara

We weaned according to the Almanac
but the mare runs the fence
end to end longing for her filly.
Moonlight flares, a searchlight
for calves who bawl across
the hills in stop and start calls
for their mothers.
Long low moans of primal loss.
My bone depth yearning for you.

NL

Camp Funston
January 18th, 1918

Sara —

To be thought of twice in one
day is really my altitude record.
As lucky as I am now, I really
believe I ought to start picking
winners or throwing dice, and add
some material emoluments to the
governments friendly contribution.

When my battery marched out
to drill this morning every man
in it must have yearned for the
day when he could have a shot
at me from some unnoticed spot

But what a splendid snappy drill it was! I never did put so much energy into commands, and those splendid big children leaped into high speed in response to the eager devil giving the commands. But at noon I had the letter which gave me your definition of "adore." If I didn't treasure that sentence so close to my heart, I could start a bit of fiction with it, and the editor would be signing a check without even bothering to read further.

And then at evening came a knock

at my door, and there stood my
hatchet-faced orderly with your other
letter. With difficulty I kept my
face in its usual mule-like repose
and laid the letter 'carelessly' upon
my table.

Now I feel as though it would always
be "the" letter to me, though Hope
whispers that I shall hold others from
you as fast in my heart.

But this letter, even more than its
predecessors, brought you to me

You, — happy eyed and joyous, were
here.

How inadequate are words when
one yearns to say, — to give utterance
to the real emotions. Perhaps they
are "splendid treasures of the tomb
in which the ages lie", but they cannot
convey for me the things I want you
to know. Thank the Gods you
understand without such artifices.

Music alone can even begin to

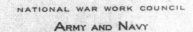

NATIONAL WAR WORK COUNCIL

ARMY AND NAVY

YOUNG MEN'S CHRISTIAN ASSOCIATIONS

"WITH THE COLORS"

2/28 — 1918

Sara—

This Christian paper was begged. I had none at all. But I am still a Pagan.

You dear. Don't worry about Emporia one bit. Just let that subject pass forever from your mind. Nobody wants Calvin but you — and nobody will ever have him but you. So the reporter frightened you did he.

Now Emporia's newspapers would really be tremendously interested in you, in the fact that you are living in Kansas City now etc. And why shouldn't they be? But don't concern yourself about the Judge and all those little worries. If he were so angry his finger nails sprouted he couldn't lift a finger in your direction. Much as I dislike

¥

The stagnant monotony of my native heath, I shall eventually have to take you back there to give you confidence.

Back there if you are white and wear shoes in the summer-time, you develope such a caste feeling that you feel superior to courts, newspapers, people and everything else.

Dont talk to the reporters at all. I have a secret feeling (that belongs to the sixteenth century) that men who make their living prying into other peoples affairs really are upon about the same plane as those who derive their income from shaving other men's beards.

And dont be unhappy or distressed. How I yearn to get you so far away that you will never hear the word Kansas mentioned, say nothing of being frightened by it.

NATIONAL WAR WORK COUNCIL

ARMY AND NAVY

YOUNG MEN'S CHRISTIAN ASSOCIATIONS

"WITH THE COLORS"

_____1917

3/

You _are_ the sort I would love
to have you. Please don't say "if"
about such things ever again.
And _I do need you._ You are my
life. You missing and I shall be
a lump of clay in France before
the year is out. You here and
I shall never know failure.

If we were not seperated you would
feel very keenly how much our
lives were mutually dependent, but
now it seems to you as though we
were not at all.

'C'est la guerre' and not us.
When it is over we shall establish
a home in which you will be
more than 50%. And we will live
a life of such sort that we
both know it all and are interested
in it all.

Pray don't feel useless or

116

of inefficient. You are the grandest thing
in mothers that exists in America,
and the loveliest sweetheart that
ever existed anywhere anytime, and
the finest, clearest-eyed girl your humbly
ever knew: and you darn as no
one else can darn, and can cook
chocolate cake wonderfully (you say),
and know what Marcus Aurelius
thought and who Horace was,
and the imagery Synge found
under thatched roofs, and you can
coax melody out of that lovely
throat in so harmonious a fashion
that it leaves me faint with
happiness, and you have a sensitive
soul and a warm heart, and a
thoroughly healthy body, and you
aren't obsessed by any religious
atavistic shackles, and you dance
like one of "the little folk," and

117

_____1917

51

swim like a mermaid, and walk
like a Weston — and kiss like
an 'houri'. So why should you
feel inefficient?

I live in hopes of seeing you
Saturday.

Mason

SARA TO JOHN MASON

By the dark limestone sink hole
now a frozen pond layered with snow,
I ache for you this Sunday.
In a war-field strewn with fallen soldiers
I thought I saw you lying there
gazing up at stars, freezing to death.
Only it is I out there, wondering
about fire, if it will ever warm me again.

NL

Sara –

Children live happy lives because they get their joy from the little incidental happenings of each day without waiting for great things. And their unhappiness is only because they do not realize the unimportance of the fact that the doll's hair came off. Unfortunately when they have lived enough to learn that it really doesn't matter if a paper doll is torn, they lose interest in the dolls, and while the little things can no longer take away happiness, nothing but great and unusual events can bring joy.

Now what a wonderful thing to find delight in the events of a normal day, and to refuse to grieve save when the real mask of Tragedy appears!

Thus far this week I have thought of nothing but you. I must be in the cavalry where one doesn't need to think—**Mason to Sara**

Tuesday morning
3/5/18

Sara —

The corrections for the day, i.e "the corrections in range and deflection when at 1000 meters above the earth the wind is coming from 28 at a rate of 7 meters per hour, the change in muzzle velocity due to temperature of powder and air" — and a lot of other numerals and formulas to be subtracted and divided, leave me quite dizzy. I write to you because you have enough maternal instinct to pretend that you think I have a brain. You are alone in the pretense.

In truth, "thou art mated with a clown.."

Thus far this week I have thought of nothing but you. I must be in the cavalry where one doesn't need to think

Then I can placidly think of you all day and harm nothing.

The watch came just now. Merci beaucoup. I was lost without it,—completely.

Am enclosing a letter from down in the Ozark mountains which interested me as a piece of excellent expression. It's terribly mis-spelled of course but the woman brings her case before you in a vivid unanswerable way. The statement, "I was always a weekly woman" is particularly vivid. Can't you see and hear her?

Today I have come around to the laughing
stage when I think of your statements
about my lack of zest and enjoyment
last week end. Was anything ever so
delightfully humorous? "I dream of you
by day and long for you by night" and
spend the time I ought to spend studying
in writing to you, and exist six days
because of the seventh — to be told that
I seem uninterested. Mother of Jesus!
What if I really were interested then?

Laughter and tears! that's why we love
the Irish. The English neither laugh nor
cry. Why haven't I more than a half
of the Celtic blood! Never mind, this
next generation you speak of will
be "three quarters bred," — out of a
thoroughbred dam by a half blooded sire."
They might show speed. Quien sabe?

4/ However we are not ready for any additional souls yet. The end of the war, and an oil well are first requisite.

Of this there can be no doubt nor any difference in viewpoint, — bless your heart.

At last I feel as though home were there and that I am just down here working. I await with all eagerness the end of the week so that I may lay aside my shovel and go back to my own colleen.

No roof in Dublin itself shelters one that is half so winsome, nor any part so lovely. Small wonder that with the memory of one pink vision glimpsed in a mirror I say "a verra proud mon."

Mason

SARA HEARS FROM JOHN MASON

You called from Kalispell,
your voice shivering through waterways –
a world vibration—I could hear
with one ear cupped to the creek.
You said you were acting like a local
at The Old Moose Saloon. Were you
the captain of the gold rush ship or
my wildcatter calling in from the mountains?
Whoever you were, I heard you.

NL

SARA LEAVES HOME

How did we launch
from here without fainting
from fear?

We sisters were sent out in dresses
to meet the men. Husbands,
employers. Straight from the convent.
They did not think much of us until later,
When we took jobs, ran their households.
Only then did they join us.

I went to meet him in my britches,
ready to ride his Cavalry mounts.
We rode in the prairie, along creeks,
under apple trees in bloom.
He began to see who I was.

Little did I know I wouldn't be going home,
wouldn't be accepted there, that I would move us
fifty-five times all by myself, with two children,
one I had kept from before, the one he adopted.
I didn't know until later I was beautiful.
What mattered was his interest in my ability.
Anyway, we rode together that day,
and many after.

NL

Sara

Sara and John Mason

Nana working polo horses

ACKNOWLEDGMENTS

My thanks to Jeanie Thompson for spending days at Tirbracken in shaping this 1917 book. Fred Smock, Katerina Stoykova-Klemer, Gill Holland, Sr., and Kay Gill read the first draft carefully and helped me along the way. Joan Rapp, a true editor, found many errors. Julie Tirpak, on her own time, has recorded and changed my drafts. Without her clear vision, I couldn't have sorted out the pages. Other writers have contributed their belief and support. I am so grateful to them.

My grandfather, John Mason Houghland, read poetry to me as a child, from his armchair early in the morning. My grandmother came from the plains and set up a household in Tennessee that could have been in the English countryside it was so cultured. She provided the knowledge that one is able to change.

The teachers who stand out among the many are Madeline Covi and Sena Naslund. Authors of the many books I read about WWI, the war that weakened Europe for the onset of WWII gave me the sense of entering the dreadful conditions, including self-serving leadership, that soldiers endured and died from. I am grateful to those good minds who helped me imagine going to war.

How would I feel as a soldier from Indiana or Kentucky headed for the wars in the desert, or the mud in France? How did John Mason feel?

Katerina Stoykova-Klemer emigrated from Bulgaria to become a publisher. She is well aware of what wars do to a country. We are so fortunate she came to Kentucky to be a publisher of poetry—that which overcomes war.

NANA LAMPTON
Goshen, Kentucky
2016

CREDITS

BIBLIOGRAPHY

The Nature of Things
Lucretius
Translated with Notes by A. E. Stallings
Introduction by Richard Jenkins
Penguin Classics
ISBN: 978-0-141-39690-3

The Sugar Pond And The Fritter Tree
Jess Wilson
Kentucke Imprints
Berea, Kentucky 40403
1981

The First World War
John Keegan
Vintage Books
2000
ISBN 978-0-375-70045-3

Every Force Evolves a Form: Twenty Essays
Guy Davenport
North Point Press
San Francisco
1987
ISBN: 0-86547-247-5

The Guns of August
Barbara W. Tuchman
With a Foreward by Robert K. Massie
A Presidio Press Book
Published by The Random House Publishing Group
ISBN: 0-345-47609-3

Camp Funston
Kim Gant
Kansapedia—Kansas Historical Society
https://www.kshs.org/kansapedia/camp-funston/16692

CPSIA information can be obtained at www.ICGtesting.com
Printed in the USA
LVOW10*1810041215

464523LV00001B/2/P